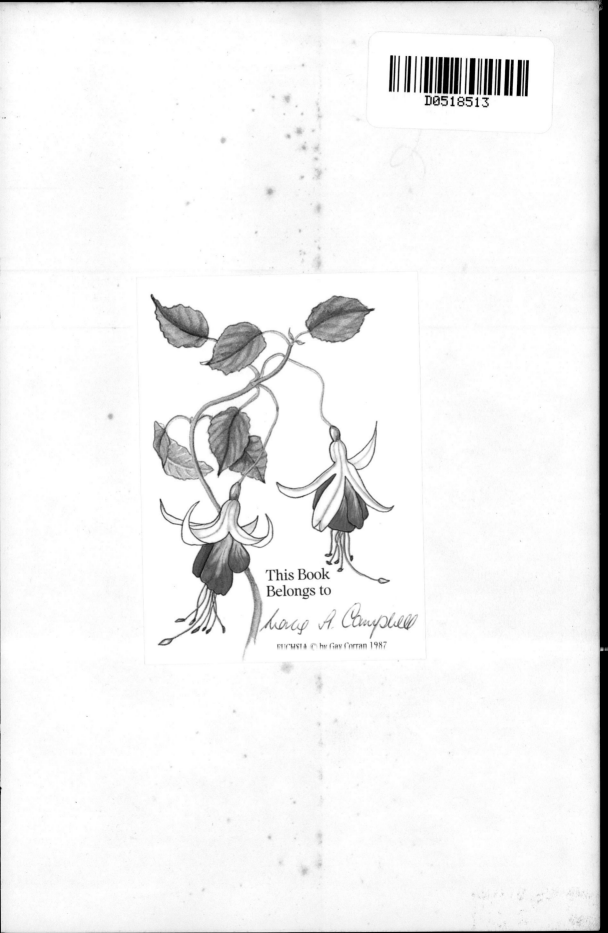

This Book
Belongs to

[signature]

FUCHSIA © by Gay Corran 1987

ATHENS

COLOUR PLATE I (Frontispiece). *Kore from the Acropolis, also known as the "Peplos Kore" because of the peplos, or Dorian woollen robe, that she wears; in the Acropolis Museum (compare plate 23). Note the formal archaic style. Much of the original colour on hair, eyes and lips has been preserved.*

ATHENS

MARTIN HÜRLIMANN

74 PICTURES IN PHOTOGRAVURE

FIVE COLOUR PLATES

AND HISTORICAL NOTES

INTRODUCTORY TEXT BY

REX WARNER

LONDON

THAMES AND HUDSON

FIRST PUBLISHED 1956

PRODUCED BY THAMES AND HUDSON LTD LONDON AND ATLANTIS VERLAG ZURICH
TEXT PRINTED IN GREAT BRITAIN BY JARROLD AND SONS LTD NORWICH
GRAVURE PLATES PRINTED BY GBR. FRETZ ZURICH
COLOUR PLATES PRINTED BY CONZETT AND HUBER ZURICH

ATHENS

People have attempted in different ways to explain the miracle of the sudden rise and the peculiar splendour of Athenian civilization. And indeed "miracle" seems an appropriate word when we reflect that in two or three generations a small people living in a small and rocky land changed the world and determined its history by their rapid and brilliant discoveries; that they not only gave us the names of the arts and sciences but in many cases achieved what is still perfection in the practical application of their discoveries. The achievement is so extraordinary and, in a sense, so complete that it may almost seem to us that Athenian civilization, like the goddess Athene herself, must have sprung fully armed into existence by means of a miraculous and inexplicable birth.

Yet we should find it impossible precisely to name the date of this birth or to imagine its circumstances. It is true that the greatest age of Athens began with the setting up of a democratic system of government, with the successes of Athenian arms in the Persian wars and with an advancing Athenian imperialism. But it is also true that neither to democracy, success in arms or imperialism can be satis- factorily attributed the tremendous and unique achievements of the Athenian intellect. Other peoples have been democratic, militarily successful and imperialistic without adding much to the cultural inheritance of mankind. Nor were Athenian theory and practice with regard to political organization and imperialist expansion always approved by the best Athenians of the great age. It should be noted also that, though the Athenians were certainly proud of themselves as innovators, they were equally proud of a long tradition. If they claimed to be "a school for Hellas" because of the novelty and success of their undertakings, they also claimed to be the oldest civilized power

in Hellas. Euripides, though an innovator himself and critic of estab-
lished ways, stresses in his praise of Athens not her inventions but
her antiquity.

> From of old the children of Erechtheus are
> Splendid, the sons of blessed gods . . .

He especially connects them with "sacred Wisdom" and with "golden
Harmony". Yet these are the same Athenians of whom, because of
their reckless enterprise and insatiable modern ambitions, Thucydides
writes, "They are by nature incapable of either living a quiet life
themselves or of allowing anyone else to do so."

These contradictions between antiquity and modernity, between
harmony and restlessness are only two out of many that might be noted.
And those who admire today what remains of ancient Athenian art,
literature and architecture will, I think, approach nearer to their
understanding if they are prepared to recognize that the perfection has
grown out of a struggle, that the balance is a balance of stress and
tension, that the miracle admits of no easy explanation.

Yet, though the achievements are eternal, they took place in time
and were the work of real people. They stand in their own right, but
they cast shadows and they evoke memories. The landscape itself,
the clear and liquid air, the mountains and the plains seem thronged
with the great ghosts of gods, of heroes and of men. We cannot question
them and we can scarcely know them; but neither can we be indifferent
to their presence, so near they seem to the grasp and apprehension of
our senses and of our minds.

Gods and goddesses whose names were unspeakable and w ose
attributes were terrific; deities of clarity, wisdom and beneficence;
unpredictable powers—all were there and, it may be said, all exist still.
It is, incidentally, neither by accident nor wholly for convenience that
those who, whether as psycho-analysts or as poets or as metaphysicians,
attempt to look behind the appearances of today, still employ in their
researches names and concepts taken from Greek mythology. Nor

6

COLOUR PLATE II. *View of the Acropolis from the
Museum Hill; Mount Lycabettus in the background.
(Compare with the view from the west shown on plate 2.)*

does it seem accidental that in those stories of the actions of the gods
which are localized in Athens we find something of the same pattern
which we shall observe everywhere in the history and achievements
of this people. We find conflict and contradiction fused together into
the making of a strange new harmony. One calls to mind, for example,
the quarrel between Athene and Poseidon, their beneficent reconciliation
and their gifts. (Athene's olive is still to be seen on the Acropolis.)
Then there is the stranger and apparently insoluble question of the
guilt or innocence of Orestes, ordered by Apollo to slay his mother
and then persecuted by the Erinyes, older powers, for having obeyed
the divine command. This question also was settled in Athens in a
court presided over by Athene and settled in such a way that the fierce
destroying avengers became known for the future as "the Kindly Ones".
Here too, at the place where now stands a railway station, the greatest
and most innocent of sinners, Oedipus, found peace, reconciliation
and a stature greater than human.

It was King Theseus who honourably gave his protection to the
aged Oedipus, and with Theseus we are already on the borders of
history and still very much in literature; for Theseus appears not only
in history and legend, but also in the work of Euripides, Sophocles,
Catullus, Ovid, Shakespeare, Racine and André Gide.

But we are still at some distance from the familiar world of men.
Little enough is known of Athens during the period when it was
ruled by kings or of how precisely the various kingdoms of Attica
were united under a single monarchy. Yet "Cyclopean" masonry can
still be seen on the Acropolis and this, together with certain names of
places and of flowers, will remind us of the antiquity of the place and
of its connexion with that strange civilization of Mycenae and of
Crete which soon after the supposed time of Theseus was to be
destroyed by Dorian invasions.

From these invasions (about 1100–1000 B.C.) Athens, perhaps
because of the poverty of her soil, appears not to have suffered greatly.

7

Monarchy, as elsewhere in Greece, was replaced by an aristocratic form of government. In the ninth and eighth centuries particularly fine "geometric" pottery was produced; but of the people themselves little enough is known. Occasionally a gleam of light comes through the darkness, as when Thucydides writes: "The Athenians were the first to give up the habit of carrying weapons [he means on all occasions] and to adopt a way of living that was more relaxed and more luxurious. In fact the elder men of the rich families who had these luxurious tastes only recently gave up wearing linen undergarments and tying their hair behind their heads in a knot fastened with a clasp of golden grass-hoppers: the same fashions spread to their kinsmen in Ionia, and lasted there among the old men for some time." But we do not know precisely when the more relaxed life first appeared (perhaps in the seventh or sixth century) and it seems likely that the luxurious fashions came from Ionia to Athens rather than from Athens to Ionia.

Certainly it was in the sixth century and under the dictatorship of the popular leader Pisistratus that Athens became for the first time an important power both materially and culturally. Athenian poetry appears in the same period, the law-giver Solon being the first poet. Now Athenian black-figured pottery begins to enjoy almost a monopoly in the Greek world; the vast temple of Olympian Zeus is part of the tyrant's building programme, though the temple remained unfinished until the time of the Emperor Hadrian. This is also the first great period of Athenian sculpture; indeed there are some who would maintain that in this respect it is the greatest period of all.

In later years, and perhaps because of the sudden and extraordinary successes of the new invention of "democracy", it became among the Athenians fashionable to decry the time when they had been ruled by "tyrants". Harmodius and Aristogeiton, the murderers of Pisistratus' son, were made into national heroes and much later on in history their example must have appealed to the sentimental or doctrinaire republi-canism of a Cato or a Brutus. In fact the rule of the "tyrant" Pisistratus

COLOUR PLATE III. *Southern section of the east front of the Parthenon, with Salamis in the back-ground.*

seems to have been both mild and enlightened. Under him (and again we note the contradiction) were developing the conditions which made democracy (the most complete democracy that has ever existed) possible. And, if Thucydides is to be believed, as he nearly always is, the motive of action for the tyrannicides was an unfortunate love affair rather than any theory of national liberation. The nation was already there, as we can see from what survives of its art and as we know from the immediate events in its history. For in this small territory there now begins a century of intellectual and artistic invention and achievement unparalleled in the history of mankind.

In this century Athens, with her new democratic constitution and with her growing strength and confidence, appears both as the liberator and as "the tyrant city", both as a rapidly and rashly expanding imperialism and as a force drawing to herself everything of distinction in the known world. Athenian enterprise and self-confidence appear together with Athenian curiosity and powers of adaptation. And above all, in every work of art or literature that survives we shall admire that peculiar Athenian clarity of outlook and certainty of expression. For here again is one of those impossible syntheses: it is as though innocence and experience were combined, as though a man rich in years, knowledge and ability were looking at the world with the eyes of a child and speaking in the accents of a god.

The century, looked at from a political or historical point of view, seems to consist of three periods, each of roughly thirty years—almost three acts or ages, of youth, of maturity and of decline. The first thirty years are dominated by the wars with Persia, the astounding successes of Athens on land and sea, the foundation of the Athenian empire in the Confederacy of Delos, the triumphant unfolding of Athenian democracy. It is an age of statesmen and generals, the age of Cleisthenes, Themistocles and Cimon, though it should not be forgotten that in 490 Aeschylus fought at Marathon and that ten years later the young Sophocles was chosen to lead the paean of victory after Salamis. The victory celebrations must have occurred in a city that had been wasted and partially destroyed by the Persians. No city has ever been rebuilt so speedily and with such splendour.

The next thirty years or so constitute what is known as "the age of Pericles". In this period Athens becomes frankly and unashamedly an imperialist power. The contributions from her allies, originally levied for supply in the war against Persia, are used to beautify the city and to increase her domination. The expansion of power is enormous. These are the times of which Pericles himself remarks, "our adventurous spirit has forced an entry into every sea and into every land", and at the close of this period he gives this advice to his fellow citizens: "that you should fix your eyes every day on the greatness of Athens as she really is, and should fall in love with her". And indeed, as he would have wished it so, Athens "as she really is" has been an object of devotion not only to the Athenians and all Hellenes but to races of men of whose existence Pericles was unaware and in continents which still remained to be discovered.

These are the years in which the buildings of the Parthenon, the Propylaea and many others were completed. In these years also were shown, in a different theatre on the same site as the existing theatre of Dionysus, the plays of Aeschylus and Sophocles and Euripides. The Athenian Phidias, born in the year of the battle of Marathon, revolutionized sculpture. Every art flourished and from all over Greece thinkers, writers and artists came to Athens, "the school of Hellas". Among those who came was the historian Herodotus who received from the Athenians a gift of money which is said to have been the largest literary award ever given to an author.

Another and a very different historian, Thucydides, had grown up in this period and had "fallen in love with" Athens. He is our chief source for the history of the last thirty years of the century and in his clear, objective, yet passionate account of the war, lasting for twenty-seven years, between Athens and Sparta, he has given the world, as

COLOUR PLATE IV. *Lecythus with white background, in the National Museum; a masterpiece of the so-called Achilles painter, active during the third quarter of the fifth century B.C., representing a warrior taking leave of a seated woman.*

he intended to do, "a possession for ever". Those who wish to see Athens "as she really is", at her best and at her worst, must read Thucydides. Yet the story of her gigantic efforts to retain and even to expand her empire, her gallantry, her cynicism, her incredible enterprise, the final disasters in which she loses her fleets, her armies, her democracy and her fortifications—this is still not the whole of the picture. During these terrible years of war, plague, revolution and collapse some of the great architectural projects were interrupted; money was needed to pay the troops and the crews of fleets. Even so, it was in this period that the Erechtheum was built and it was in these years also that were produced the greatest plays of Sophocles and Euripides. Aristophanes too in his comedies developed a style of writing unique in the history of the world. Apart altogether from the artistic merits of his plays, it should be noted that never before or since has a State been able to permit such devastating criticism on the public stage of her leaders in times of desperate emergency.

Nevertheless the end of the fifth century seems the end of an epoch. True enough that within ten years Athens had regained her democracy and her fleet. Yet something had gone from the world for ever. The comedy of Aristophanes did not survive in the new world. It was replaced by a comedy of manners, something "more civilized" perhaps, but less robust. And in 399, exactly a hundred years from the time when Athens had first intervened against Persia in the cause of freedom, an Athenian court condemned to death Socrates, who more than any other had developed that freedom of speech and thought on which the Athenians of earlier generations had particularly prided themselves. Still, it would be unfair to suggest that the condemnation of Socrates was characteristic of the times. The fourth century, with Plato and Aristotle both teaching and writing in Athens, is the great age of philosophy. It is also, with Demosthenes and others, the great age of oratory; and in sculpture the Athenian Praxiteles found a new style of delicacy and of charm. Nor, if we consider the career of Xenophon, can we find anything lacking in Athenian dexterity, courage and versatility. It was not until the year 322, after Alexander's conquests in the east, that Athens was finally crushed by the forces of Macedon, never again to appear as a strong independent power.

From that time until her real independence in modern days Athens has continued to conquer her conquerors and to enlighten the world. If the buildings and achievements of the age of Pericles remain the great glory of the city, there are many other glories in subsequent ages, many other ghosts that can be evoked.

It was in 146 B.C. that Athens, with the rest of Greece, came under the power of the Roman Republic, and the effect of Athenian culture on Rome, deplored as it was by Cato the elder, cannot be over-emphasized, though in the first century of Roman rule Athens herself narrowly escaped destruction. At the time when Julius Caesar was a boy the city, unfortunately for herself, joined in the general revolt of the east from Rome which was led by Mithridates. She was subdued, after a terrible siege, by the formidable and relentless Sulla who, when Athenian envoys came to him and, in the hope of obtaining some honourable terms, began to speak about the Persian wars and the glories of the past, is said to have replied: "You can give up your speech-making, my friends. Rome sent me to Athens to crush rebels, not to learn ancient history." In the subsequent sack of the city, if we are to believe Plutarch, the population was almost exterminated. "There was no numbering the slain; the amount is to this day conjectured only from the space of ground overflowed with blood." After a time Sulla is said to have ordered a cessation of the massacre and, "making some honourable mention of the ancient Athenians", to have declared that he would forgive the living, such as remained, for the sake of the dead.

As had happened before and was to happen after, Athens recovered in an incredibly short space of time. Seven or eight years after the sack of the city by Sulla's legions we find Cicero there, eagerly attending lectures in philosophy and rhetoric. A little later, Pompey the Great, returning from his triumphs in the east, employed some of his spoils in beautifying the city and in rewarding the eloquence of her philosophers. It may be said with some justice and some pathos that the Athens of Pericles had now become a mere university; but it must be remembered that universities have a more lasting influence than armies or fleets and also that Athens is the mother of every university in the western world.

Under the empire Athens long remained an important centre of learning and education. She suffered from the depredations of the Emperor Nero who, like Lord Elgin, defaced the Parthenon, though less extensively than the British peer; and she was particularly favoured by another "intellectual" Emperor, Hadrian, whose building operations can compare in extent with the buildings undertaken in the ages of Pisistratus and of Pericles. Hadrian added a whole new quarter to the city near where his arch still stands, and it was Hadrian who finally dedicated the great temple to Olympian Zeus, begun by Pisistratus so many years before.

It was late in the day, indeed already almost a piece of antiquarianism, to be dedicating temples to Zeus. New faiths, among them Christianity, were beginning to spread through the empire. St Paul had already preached in Athens at the spot where Athene was said to have reconciled Orestes and his pursuers. It seems, however, that the early Church in Athens was of minor importance, nor even in later times when Christianity became the religion of the State and Athens passed under the control of the Byzantine Emperors did the new faith leave traces so numerous as those to be found, for example, at Salonica. Perhaps this was to be expected in a city which had thriven for so long on profane philosophy. Indeed, it would seem that the schools of philosophy did not acquiesce lightly in the new régime. Julian, before he became Emperor and Apostate, spent a pleasant period of exile in Athens in the year A.D. 355, and he was initiated in the mysteries of Eleusis. It was natural for him in later years to become a benefactor to the city which of all others could be represented as the great glory of the ancient gods. Yet these gods were not to be reanimated in this way, and even the Delphic oracle was reluctant to speak in Julian's lost cause.

Forty years after Julian's residence in the city Athens and the rest of Greece were overrun by Alaric and his Goths. Whether or not Alaric burned down the temple at Eleusis, it is certain that the Gothic invasion marks the end of the Eleusinian mysteries and also of Athens as an important cultural centre in the ancient world. Even at this time, it is said, she was less famous for her schools of philosophy than for her trade in honey.

Some centuries later her decayed fortifications were restored by Justinian, but no great buildings arose in Athens like those of Salonica, Constantinople and other cities of the eastern empire. Instead, she was despoiled of her own works of art in order to beautify other capitals.

After the Goths the Crusaders. The sack of Constantinople in 1204 was the beginning of the end of the empire, and before the western Christians burst into the city to pillage and to massacre, one of the greatest examples of Athenian art, the giant statue of Athene which then stood in the Forum of Constantinople but was made by Phidias in the time of Pericles, was, to quote Mr Steven Runciman, "Hacked to pieces by a drunken mob, because the goddess seemed to be beckoning to the invaders."

For more than two hundred years Frankish Dukes of Athens held out against the Turk, but in the middle of the fifteenth century began the Turkish occupation which lasted until the early nineteenth century, except for a brief period of Venetian rule (1687–90), the only mark of which to remain is the partial destruction of the Parthenon.

The rest is modern history and it is not a history to be overlooked. Modern events too will show Athens to be still indestructible, still brilliant and still wise. The place is eternal. Anywhere, almost, one may stand back and perceive this to be so.

It has often seemed to me, for example, that in the monastery at Daphne, near Athens, one is well placed to imagine the length, the

14

COLOUR PLATE V. *Cape Sunium, east part of the temple of Poseidon (continues left side of plate 69).*

continuity and the revolutions of this civilization. Near Daphne is the hill where on a golden throne Xerxes sat and watched the destruction of his fleet in the bay of Salamis, and across the waters of the bay is the old religious centre of Eleusis. On the rocky ground of Daphne itself once stood a temple of Apollo. This temple was destroyed about the year A.D. 400 and in the course of the next two centuries the first Christian church was built on the site. The present church with its mosaics dates from the end of the eleventh century. It has been inhabited both by Orthodox monks and by Cistercians who were installed there by a Frankish Duke of Athens after the place had been sacked by the Crusaders. This too is part of the Athenian heritage and a work of perfect art shaped in conflict, revolution, unceasing enterprise and endeavour. Over this ground have passed the troops of Xerxes and of Alexander, of Sulla and Mithridates, of Alaric and Justinian; it has been ravaged by Persians, Spartans, Romans, Crusaders, Turks and Nazis.

The storm and stress, the contradictions and the extremities of Athenian civilization are perhaps particularly to be emphasized if we are to understand the full glory of the "golden harmony" and her peace. For in this conflux and effervescence of time the achievements, in their full splendour, are as nearly timeless as any creations of man. They are the achievements of real men, of real flesh and blood. There is nothing deceptive in this brilliant air, nothing weak, nothing sentimental. We admire as we must, and of all loves and admirations, that which we feel for Athens may be the purest. So Gide writes in his journal: "Why go to any effort? There is nothing intense about my joy. I am so little surprised to be here. Everything seems to me so familiar. I seem so natural to myself here. My infatuation fills this known landscape; I recognize everything; I am 'at home': this is Greece."

Athens is still the home and the challenge, the inspiration and the deep calm, the energy and the harmony, "dear city of Cecrops", the wonder of the world.

From Lycabettus, the hill of St George, 900 feet high, one looks west-wards over the modern town to the Parthenon-crowned Acropolis, the port of Piraeus and the Gulf of Athens. On the left, the old royal palace (see plate 58).

When Athens was made the capital of the Kingdom of Greece after liberation from the Turks in 1834, it became one of the most important trading centres of the Mediterranean. Its over 800,000 inhabitants make up a good tenth of the entire population of the country.

The Acropolis seen from the west (cf. colour plate II). In the foreground, the rocky slope of Museum Hill; on the right, at the foot of the limestone rock of the Acropolis, 507 feet high, the walls of the Odeum of Herodes Atticus (plate 33), whence the Stoa Eumenia, on the right, leads to the Theatre of Dionysus. Dominant on the summit of the Acropolis, the Parthenon; on the left, the Propylaea; beyond, the Erechtheum.

The Acropolis or "high city" of Athens was once the fortified seat of the rulers and of the State sanctuaries, and was surrounded by a Cyclopean wall. The buildings erected by the tyrant Pisistratus and others in the sixth century B.C. were destroyed by the Persians in 480 B.C. Rebuilding was undertaken by Themistocles and Cimon, but it was Pericles who raised the incomparable marble structures on the site that by then housed only the sanctuaries and was dedicated in particular to Pallas Athene, the city's guardian deity. The colossal statue of Athene Promachus was erected c. 449 B.C. by Phidias from the Persian loot; the Parthenon was built in 448–432; the Propylaea in 437–432; then the Temple of Nike, and c. 421 the Erechtheum.

Already towards the end of antiquity, the Acropolis, having lost its religious significance, was robbed of its movable works of art; the Turks made it into a fortress and erected dwelling-houses on it; sieges caused further destruction. The task of freeing and reconstructing the ancient sites, begun in the nineteenth century, still continues.

The west approach to the Acropolis, seen from the north-west. On the right, two pylons from Roman times; between them, the present approach through the Beulé Gate, so called after the French archaeologist who discovered this way under the Turkish bastions. Further up the slope, the Temple of Nike. In the left foreground, above the corner-wall built by Themistocles, the 29-feet-high pedestal of Hymettus marble that once bore a statue of Agrippa, but is itself probably of earlier date. On the right, the west approach to the Propylaea (plate 5); on the left, the bare outer wall of the north wing, which according to Pausanias' description housed the Pinacotheca or picture gallery.

4

View from the west portico of the Propylaea towards the Temple of Nike in the south-west (plate 7).

5

View from the steps leading to the Propylaea towards the west portico and the Pinacotheca.

6

View from the west portico of the Parthenon towards the east front of the Propylaea; in the background, the north-west suburbs, the Attic Plain and the Aegaleus Mountains. The Propylaea were begun by the architect Mnesicles in 437 B.C. and by the beginning of the Peloponnesian war in 432 the work was almost completed. In addition to Pentelic marble, bluish marble from Eleusis was used to heighten the effect of individual features. Already in antiquity this gate with its central colonnades and two wings was admired no less than the

Parthenon itself. The gate was preserved in its original state until the thirteenth century, when additions began to be made particularly by the Turks, who made it the site of a powder-magazine, which blew up in 1656. Other acts of destruction and of looting followed, the last during the siege of 1827. In 1836 Pittakis began to free the ancient ruins; in 1875 the so-called Frankish tower was removed at the expense of H. Schliemann; and the restorations carried out by N. Balanos in 1909–17 enable us to admire today what has been preserved, in particular the east front with its six columns, 27 feet 7 inches high.

7

The Temple of Nike, east aspect. According to an inscription dating from the fifth century B.C., the temple of Athene Nike (Athene as goddess of victory), also erroneously known as Nike apteros, was planned by the architect Callicrates and built at about the same time as the Propylaea. The massive porous base is 26 feet high. The little Pentelic marble temple—a so-called amphiprostyle tetrastyle in plan —measures only 26 feet, 10 inches by 17 feet 8 inches. Both the west front (plate 3) with its wide view and the east front, which faces the Parthenon, have porticoes, each with four graceful Ionic columns 13 feet high. Over the triple architrave a 17-inches-high frieze with reliefs of gods (the heads are missing) and combatants extends for a length of $85\frac{1}{2}$ feet around the building. Lord Elgin took four blocks of the frieze from what was at the time a heap of rubble; and these have been replaced by casts. The statue of the goddess in the interior of the temple held a pomegranate in the right, and a helmet in the left hand.

The temple was destroyed in 1687 to make room for a Turkish bastion. The pieces were reassembled in 1835–6 by the German archaeologist Ludwig Ross assisted by the architects Schaubert and Hansen. Between 1935 and 1939 the temple was once again dismantled, since its base showed cracks, and then put together again.

25

The Temple of Nike, detail of south-east corner showing the recently added fragment of the gable.

Marble relief, now in the Acropolis Museum with other fragments, from the frieze that ran along three sides of the breastwork at
the edge of the terrace of the Temple of Nike. The frieze portrays Nike
goddesses (goddesses of victory) erecting trophies and offering sacrifices
before Athene, who sits on a rock. The block which we have photographed shows a winged Nike leading one of the bulls to the place
of sacrifice. It was probably carved after the naval victory won by
Alcibiades in 408/407 B.C. The fragment was found by Ross in 1835.

The resolution to build the Parthenon and thus to glorify the city-state and its deities for all time by a new and more splendid monument was reached immediately after the end of the Persian wars in 448 B.C. The work was carried out in 447–432 B.C. under Pericles; to Phidias fell the artistic supervision, while Iktinos and Callicrates were the architects. The name, Parthenon (Chamber of the Maidens), originally applied only to a part of the building the whole of which was known to the Athenians as "the great temple" or "the temple".

The temple, a Doric peripteral octastyle, stands on a stylobate of three steps also of Pentelic marble, and this in turn rests on a porous base. The narrow sides have eight columns, the long sides seventeen, their average height being 33 feet 9 inches and their diameter almost 6 feet 6 inches. On the lowest step the building measures just over 235 feet by 110 feet. Against a red background the sculptures of the east gable portrayed the birth of Athene, those of the west gable the victory of the goddess over Poseidon. The walled interior, or cella, was raised two steps above the level of the colonnade. It was divided by a partition wall into the eastern Hecatompedon, where stood Phidias' famous gold and ivory statue of Athene Parthenos, and a smaller western room, the Parthenon or Chamber of the Maidens, which was the State treasury.

10 West front and north side, with Propylaea in right foreground.

11 Columns of north side, with cella wall on right.

12 East front (cf. colour plate III).

13 East to west view of the interior, with remains of cella wall (extant only on west side).

14 View from east room towards the Erechtheum in the north.

15–16 Youths bearing pitchers and others leading a sacrificial animal, from the Panathenaic Procession depicted in the north frieze. In the Acropolis Museum.

15

17

18

The Parthenon frieze, 3 feet 3 inches high and 520 feet long, which ran along the upper edge of the cella wall, was designed by Phidias and executed in his workshop. Many of the marble slabs were removed and taken to London by Lord Elgin at the beginning of the nineteenth century and are in the British Museum. Smaller fragments are in Paris (Louvre) and in the Vatican, but some of the most beautiful have remained in Athens and are in the Acropolis Museum.

The frieze portrays the procession of the Greater Panathenaea, the national festival of Attica, which was celebrated every four years.

17 A group of old men from the north section of the frieze. In the Acropolis Museum.

18 Fragment depicting chariots with apobates, warriors in arms, who jumped on and off during the drive. On the right, a festival orator recoiling from an oncoming team.

The Erechtheum, the latest in date of the Acropolis buildings, was built immediately next to the old temple of Athene of Pisistratean times, which had been destroyed by the Persians, and was to provide a new sanctuary for the ancient image of the city's guardian deity. The irregularity of plan was due not only to religious considerations but to the downwards slope of the site to the west and north. On the north and east sides there are porticoes with Ionic columns, on the south the Korai (Porch of the Maidens). The temple was the sanctuary of Athene Polias and Erechtheus-Poseidon and was built on the spot where the goddess had been victorious in contest against Poseidon. The temple also contained a shrine to Erechtheus, a legendary king of Athens. Work on the temple was begun after the peace of Nikias in 421 B.C., interrupted shortly before completion during the years of crisis in 413–411 and finished c. 406, but restoration after a fire in the same year lasted until 395. In Byzantine times it was converted into a church and in 1463 into the harem of the Commander of the Turkish garrison. In 1837 restoration was begun, and virtually concluded in 1909.

Coming from the west one sees the exterior, ornamented with half-columns, of the narrow west room, under which a salt well was situated, with the north portico on the left and the Korai on the right.

19

Erechtheum: three of the six columns, 21 feet 4·6 inches high, of the east portico; behind them, the now bare interior and the west wall. Behind the east portico lay the cella of Athene Polias, where stood her ancient statue in olive wood; next to this, the Erechtheum proper, which consisted of two chambers presumably containing altars to Hephaestus and the legendary hero Butos; and the west room, the Prostomeum.

Erechtheum, Porch of the Maidens: the six figures of maidens, or Korai, 7 feet 5·7 inches high, that support the superstructure stand on a base 8 feet 5·4 inches high. The second Kore from the left is a cast of the original in the British Museum.

In 1853, when French archaeologists had carried out the work of reassembly, Charles Ernest Beulé, the discoverer of the Propylaea, wrote as follows about these much admired figures:

"What is remarkable about the maidens of the Erechtheum is that they not only have the plasticity of sculpture but also a monumental quality, so that their relationship to the mass and form of the whole building is harmonious. The two art forms, which in modern times are often separated, were always closely linked by the Greeks, the sculptor's work seeming to be subordinated to the architect's yet at the same time finding an effective setting therein. And from this wise co-operation between sculptor and architect resulted a synthesis that had all the consummate perfection to which art aspires. In size the caryatids are considerably larger than life, but not to such an extent as to appear massive and superhuman like colossal figures: they are conceived within the limits of reality. Their bearing is serene and strong and has nothing of the superhuman effort with which the Atlantes figures at Agrigentum stretch upwards their arms to ease the load on their heads. They bear their burden of marble with grace and dignity, as their living sisters once bore the pitchers that they filled each day at the well of Klepsydra. . . ."

Kore, in the Acropolis Museum. One of the most beautiful of the figures of girls, carved mainly during the last quarter of the sixth century, that have been found on the Acropolis and tell of the splendour of the last phase of archaic art in Pisistratean times. The marble figure, 3 feet high, shows traces of painting. The elaborately folded chiton (dress) and cloak and the graceful pose are Ionic in contrast to the earlier Kore on colour plate I, wearing the Doric peplos and still in Attic archaic style.

Head of the so-called Critius boy, in the Acropolis Museum. The head, found in 1888 among the Persian rubble on the Acropolis, was identified by H. Schrader as belonging to the torso, which had been excavated in 1865.

This is probably the dedicatory statue of a boy victorious in contest dating from the beginning of the Persian wars (c. 490–480 B.C.). The general consensus of opinion is that it is from the workshop of Critius and Nesiotes at Athens. It is probably one of the first examples of the Early Classical youthful, ideal hero-type.

Marble relief with figures of Athene and Samian Hera shaking hands; underneath, the text of the treaty concluded in 405 B.C. between Athens and Samos. From the Acropolis Museum. This museum contains only items found on the Acropolis, and thus gives a uniquely concentrated impression of Attic art during its greatest period. Some of the works of art stored during the Second World War were afterwards provisionally housed in the National Museum. The arrangement of the interior of the replanned Museum at the east end of the Acropolis hill was begun in 1955.

Relief dedicated to Athene, known as "mourning Athene". From the Acropolis. In the Acropolis Museum. The goddess, who leans on a lance, looks musingly at a boundary stone. The Parian marble shows remains of paint, c. 460, presumably by the great sculptor Myron.

27–28

Views over Athens from the top of the Acropolis.

Upper photograph: Lycabettus in the north-east background (from where the photograph for plate I was taken); on the left, amidst the confusion of houses of the modern town centre, the cupola-crowned metropolitan church (the cathedral), built in 1840–55 from the rubble of seventy small churches and chapels that were taken down; on the right, the old royal palace (see plate 58).

Lower photograph: view east and south-east. On the left, behind the Roman Olympeum, and half concealed by Mount Ardettus (432 feet) the antique Stadium, holding 70,000, which was completely renewed in 1896–1906 for the reintroduction of the Olympic Games. In the background, Mount Hymettus, which rises to a height of 3,338 feet.

29

30

From the east end of the Acropolis one can look across the north slope, and the small number of primitive dwelling-houses still at its foot, toward the Theseum, in front of which lies the Agora, excavated from beneath the town-quarter that stood on its site. Above left, a part of the wall built by Cimon near the ancient site of the so-called Erech-theus-palace, the seat of the legendary kings of Athens.

30

The Theatre of Dionysus lies at the foot of the steep south slope of the Acropolis, in the sacred Precincts of Dionysus Eleuthereus. The tiers of seats, forming a semicircle, are built into the slope. The earliest theatre, where the first play by Thespis is said to have been performed in 534 B.C., was situated in the Agora; the present site was chosen for the new theatre of 490, which did not, however, assume its final form until the orchestra was reconstructed and an auditorium in stone erected in the fourth century.

The Theatre of Dionysus.

The theatre in which the plays of Aeschylus, Sophocles, Euripides and Aristophanes were first acted stood on the present site but the auditorium that framed the circular orchestra was still of wood; the orchestra was occupied by both chorus and actors; and the stage background, representing a façade with three doors, was put up when required. During the time of the orator Lycurgus (338–326) the work of remodelling in stone was completed, but considerable further alterations were made during Roman times, particularly under Nero and Hadrian. The semicircular "Theatron" could accommodate 14–17,000 spectators, its seventy-eight tiers being divided into three sections. The sixty-seven thrones of the first row (plate 31), reserved for priests and other persons of authority, are of marble; the central throne was occupied by the Priest of Dionysus.

Plate 32 shows the façade of the stage with sculptures from the time of Nero. It was during this time that the stage was remodelled into a raised platform for the actors. The figures represent scenes from the legend of Dionysus.

The Odeum of Herodes Atticus at the foot of the south-west slope of the Acropolis was built by the rich Claudius Herodes Atticus (A.D. 101–177) in memory of his elegant Roman wife, Appia Annia Regilla. When Pausanias, that Baedeker of antiquity, visited Athens in A.D. 161 the building had not yet been erected, but he gives an account of it on a later occasion. The roof of the Odeum was of cedar wood, its seating capacity 5,000 and it was used among other purposes for musical performances. With its largely preserved three-storeyed façade in Roman round-arch style it is one of the most impressive monuments of the time of the Emperors. Today the building with its tiers of seats forming a semicircle is frequently used for open-air performances.

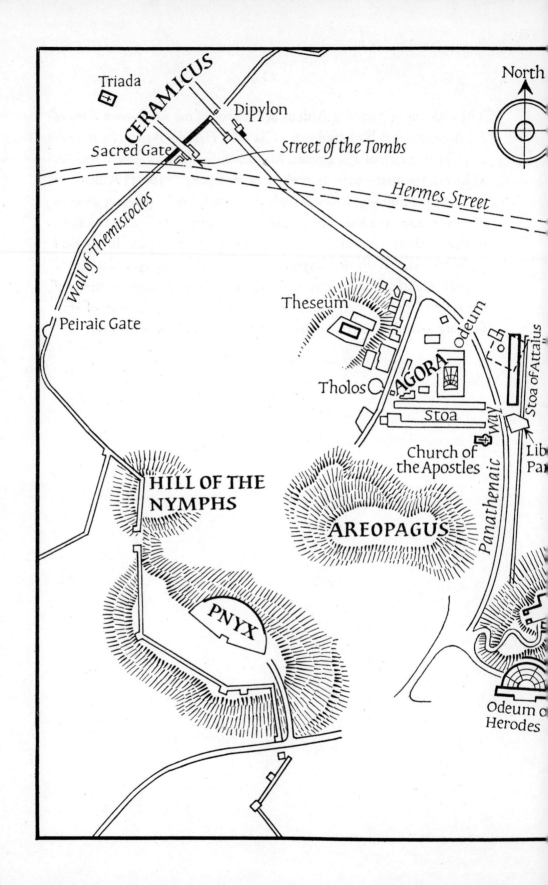

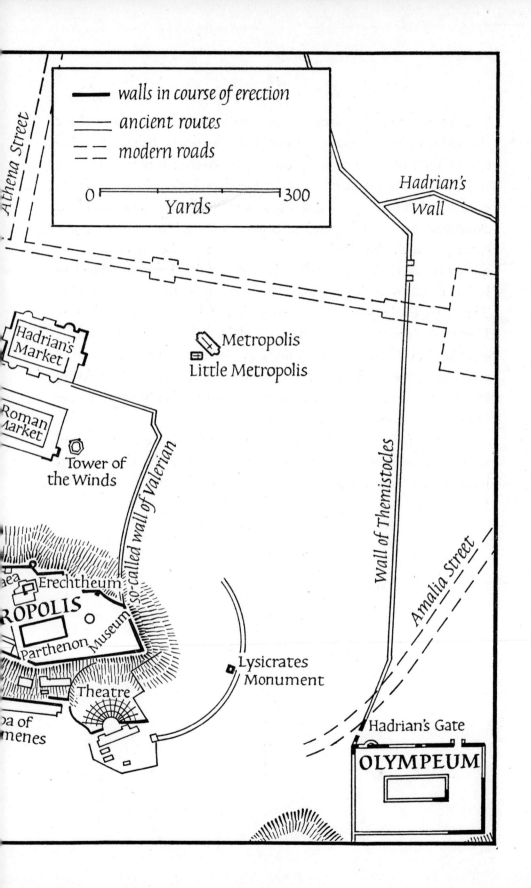

Athena Street

walls in course of erection
ancient routes
modern roads

0   Yards   300

Hadrian's
Wall

Metropolis
Little Metropolis

Hadrian's
Market

Roman
Market

Tower of
the Winds

Wall of Themistocles

Amalia Street

so-called wall of valerian

Erechtheum

aea

ROPOLIS

Parthenon

Museum

Lysicrates
Monument

Theatre

a of
menes

Hadrian's Gate

OLYMPEUM

34

The Agora, or market-place, was situated in the north-west area of the Acropolis and was the centre of public life in ancient Athens. Excavation of the site was begun by the Greek Archaeological Society in 1859, and in 1896-7 members of the German Archaeological Institute contributed to the work. But it was as a result of the excavations of the American School of Classical Studies during the thirties of this century—which involved taking down an entire modern town-quarter at vast expense—that the whole area of the Agora could be laid bare and Athens enriched with yet another important relic of antiquity. The work, carried out under the direction of Lesly Shear and later of Homer A. Thompson, was interrupted in 1940-6 but was virtually completed by 1955. The many finds, evidence of thousands of years of civilization, the gold objects ranging from Mycenaean to Christian, have been assembled to form a collection housed since September 1956 in the newly re-erected Stoa of Attalus.

The marble figure of a floating Nike which we have photographed is perhaps the most beautiful piece of sculpture of the Classical age found on the Agora. It is slightly less than life-size and dates from the fifth century.

35

Figure of a woman carrying water found on the site of a well in the Agora; probably a marble copy made in the second century A.D. after an earlier original dating from the fifth century B.C.

Through the excavation of the Agora the Temple of Hephaestus, known as the "Theseum", standing on the hill to the south, has regained its dominant position. It was built at the same time as the Parthenon, likewise of Pentelic marble, and is an exceptionally well preserved example of a Doric temple. In the fifth century it was converted into a church dedicated to St George.

36 Shows the west portico with the four interior of its six columns, just over 19 feet high. Over the entrance to the cella, emphasized by two interior columns, the frieze with reliefs depicting the battle of the Lapiths and Centaurs.

37 In the foreground, the foundations of the Tholos, a round building constructed in 470 B.C. on the west side of the Agora and altered during Roman times. In Classical times it was the meeting-place of the fifty Prytanei or presidents of the Council, a number of whom resided permanently in it. In the background, the Theseum.

38 View from the east side of the Agora westwards to the Theseum. On the left, the north entrance of the Odeum. This music hall was built by Agrippa, the son-in-law of Augustus, c. 15 B.C. After the collapse of the roof in the second century A.D. it was partially rebuilt, six piers with colossal figures of Giants and Tritons being placed along the north façade. These have been partly re-erected (cf. plate 46).

36

The little church of the Holy Apostles stands at the south-east corner of the Agora, at the foot of the Acropolis. The large nineteenth-century west addition was taken down in 1954 by the American School during their work on the Agora, and the style of the eleventh-century Byzantine building has thus been reimbued with its full significance. In the foregound, the foundation walls of the Library of Pantainos, built during the second century A.D. Its colonnade bordered the Panathenaic Way, south of the Stoa of Attalus.

The Horologium, known as the Tower of the Winds, and in the Middle Ages as the Grave of Socrates, was built in the first century B.C. by Andronicus of Cyrrhus in Macedonia. The marble octagon has a diameter of 26 feet 8 inches and is 41 feet 7 inches high (including the base); it used to contain a water-clock. The sides of the tower correspond to the eight winds, whose symbolic winged figures are represented on the frieze. On the right, over the north-east portico, bearded Caicias, shaking hailstones from his shield. In the centre, facing east, youthful Apeliotes, bearing fruits and ears of corn. On the left, facing south-east, Eurus wrapped in a cloak. On the remaining sides, Notos, Lips, Zephyrus, Skiron and Boreas. Below the figures are marks for the sun-dials.

The Roman Agora, at the foot of the north slope of the Acropolis, seen from west to east. On the right, the Tower of the Winds; in the left background, Mount Lycabettus.

The market-place, which was laid out during the time of the first Emperors, measured 364 feet by 312 feet, and surrounded an inner courtyard, 267 feet by 185 feet, paved with marble and enclosed by a colonnade.

The main cemetery of ancient Athens was in the Ceramicus, just out-side the Dipylon, the principal town gate, where the road led to Eleusis, Megara and Thebes. Some of the funerary monuments of the fifth and fourth centuries B.C., among which are masterpieces of Attic sculpture, are now in the National Museum.

42 The fourth-century monument of Hegeso, representing a woman adorning herself, and a servant woman.

43 Monument in the form of a slender marble vessel, a so-called Lutrophorus, with a relief depicting a man and a woman on the bowl. Below the volutes of the tall handles is a motif of acanthus leaves. In the background, the Aya Trias church from the nine-teenth century.

44 One of the stelae, now in the National Museum, from the graves outside the Dipylon. The inscription refers to Mika and Dion. The seated woman gives her right hand to the young man and holds a mirror in the other, c. 440.

ΜΙΚΑ   ΔΙΩΝ

45

46

47

The monument of Lysicrates was one of many, erected to the memory of victors in the Dionysian contests, that bordered both sides of the street leading from the town to the Theatre of Dionysus. It owes its preservation to the fact that from 1669 until into the nineteenth century it formed part of a Capuchin monastery. The cylindrical structure of Pentelic marble with its six Corinthian columns is 21 feet 2 inches high and stands on a base 13 feet high. The roof consists of a single block of marble; the frieze tells a story from the legend of Dionysus. The monument, which dates from the fourth century B.C., bears the inscription: "Lysicrates of Kikynna, son of Lysitheides, was choregos; the tribe Akamantis gained the victory with a chorus of boys; Theon played the flute; Lysiades, an Athenian, trained the chorus, Euainetos was archon."

46

Head of a Triton, from one of the colossal figures along the north façade of the Odeum in the Agora (plate 38). The head, dating from the second century A.D., is a copy of the head of Poseidon in the west gable of the Parthenon.

47

Figure of Silenus, on the plinth of the Roman stage building in the Theatre of Dionysus (plate 32).

48

Sepulchral monument with the figure of a bull in Pentelic marble, from the lot of Dionysus Kollytos (fourth century B.C.) in the cemetery outside the Dipylon (plates 42–44).

The Arch of Hadrian was built by the Emperor or his successor at the entrance to the new quarter added by him (the Hadrianopolis or Novae Athenae). The south-east façade shown in the photograph bears the inscription: "This is the city of Hadrian and not of Theseus." The inscription on the façade facing the Acropolis reads: "This is Athens, the former city of Theseus." The Pentelic marble gateway with Corinthian columns is 58 feet 6 inches high.

50-51

The Olympeum, the Temple of Olympian Zeus south-east of the Arch of Hadrian, was begun in Pisistratean times and although only built as far as the foundation walls was already on a magnificent scale. Building operations were continued by Antiochus IV, King of Syria in 175–164 B.C., but it was Hadrian who completed the enormous temple, dedicating it in A.D. 131/132 during the Pan-hellenic Festival. His statue was placed next to the gold and ivory image of the Olympian god.

Of the 104 marble columns sixteen have been preserved, and fifteen are still standing. They are 56 feet high, with a diameter of 4 feet 10 inches at the top and 5 feet 6 inches at the bottom.

Geometric-style funerary krater 4 feet high dating from the eighth century when figured ornamentation was first introduced. From the cemetery outside the Dipylon. The composition represents the funeral group; above right, the dead man on a four-legged bier, drawn on a two-wheeled chariot.

Plates 52 to 56, as well as plates 44 and 74, illustrate the quality of the exhibits in the National Archaeological Museum at Athens. Although in late antiquity and in the early nineteenth century collectors of Greek art-treasures did not scruple to take away whatever was movable, the Athens Museum is today unrivalled in its wealth of original works produced during the flowering of art up to the fourth century B.C. Finds made during the last century, when their removal was prohibited by law, and in recent years, have altered fundamentally our ideas of Greek art, which in Goethe's and Winckelmann's days had still been largely determined by late antique copies.

Kouros 6 feet 11·5 inches high found at Melos, by an island sculptor active during the middle of the sixth century. This is one of the later of the magnificent archaic figures of youths of this type in the National Museum; the sensitiveness of the carving gives the statue a less hieratic and formal appearance.

54

Poseidon (or Zeus ?), bronze figure somewhat over life-size dating from *c.* 460 B.C., recovered in 1928 from the sea near Cape Artemiseum, the northern tip of Euboea. This is one of the most magnificent originals from the time of the Persian wars, when the famous group by Critius and Nesiotes—of which only copies survive—of the "Liberators", Harmodius and Aristogeiton, was created.

The Anticythera Ephebe, bronze figure somewhat over life-size dating from *c.* 340 B.C. and found in the sea near Anticythera (a small island between Cythera, south of Laconicus, and the western tip of Crete) in 1900. On the evidence of renewed research after the Second World War the fragments were re-set into their original position.

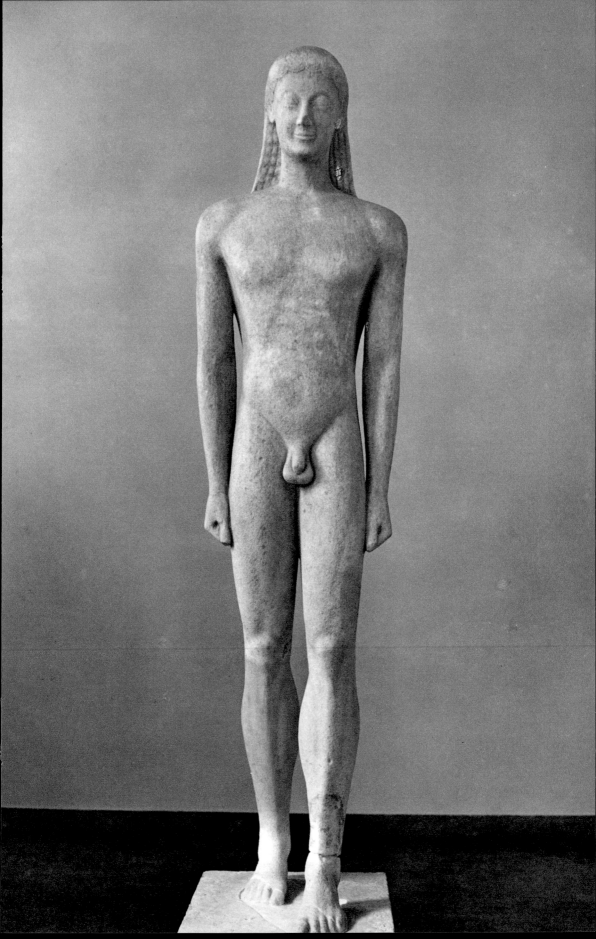

Lecythus with white ground by the "Reed Master" active in Athens c. 430–400 B.C., depicting a dead youth sitting in front of his tomb- stone, and a pious visitor to the tomb.

The Academy, situated in one of the main modern thoroughfares, was built in the nineteenth century entirely of Pentelic marble and is a faithful imitation of the architecture of ancient Athens. The plans were designed by the Danish architect Theophil von Hansen, whose brother was responsible for the university building of 1837; the group in the main gable depicting the birth of Athene, as well as the figures of Athene and Apollo standing on the two columns, and the two seated figures of Plato and Socrates are by the Greek sculptor Dhrosus. The funds were provided by the Viennese Baron Sina.

58

The memory of the first Bavarian royal house of the new kingdom of Greece is preserved in the former royal palace, now the seat of Parliament. The building is the work of the philhellenic Munich school of architects and was built in 1834–8 of Pentelic marble and limestone after plans by Friedrich von Gärtner, which had been preceded by a design by Leo von Klenzes. The funds were provided partly by Ludwig I of Bavaria, the father of Otto I (1832–62), the first king of the Hellenes.

The guard at the monument to the Unknown Soldier in front of the Parliament building is kept by Evzones, members of Highland Regiments, whose gala uniform, consisting of red pointed cap, richly embroidered jerkin, white pleated "Fustella", reminiscent of a Scottish kilt, and pointed shoes with large tassels, preserves the old national costume deriving from the Albanian Tosk.

60

The Little Metropolis, also known as Panayia Gorgopicus or Ayus
Elefthereus, dating from the ninth century, stands in front of the south
side of the Metropolitan Church. Its small size, which gives it the
appearance of a private chapel, is surprising in a cathedral church, but
is not unusual among Greek churches. It contains numerous fragments
of reliefs from earlier antique and Byzantine monuments.

61

The monastery of Daphne with its cupola-crowned church, situated on
the road from Athens to Eleusis, was built in 1082–1105. During the
thirteenth–fifteenth centuries it belonged to the Cistercians, who made
the Gothic additions.

62

The church of Capnicaraea, situated in Hermes Street in the centre of
Athens, is an eleventh-century Byzantine building, to which later
additions were made on the south and north.

63

The cupola of the Byzantine monastery church of Daphne (plate 61)
is ornamented with mosaics on a gold ground dating from the eleventh
century. In the centre, Christ Pantocrator; Moses, David, Isaiah and
Solomon are among the smaller figures seen in this (eastward) view.

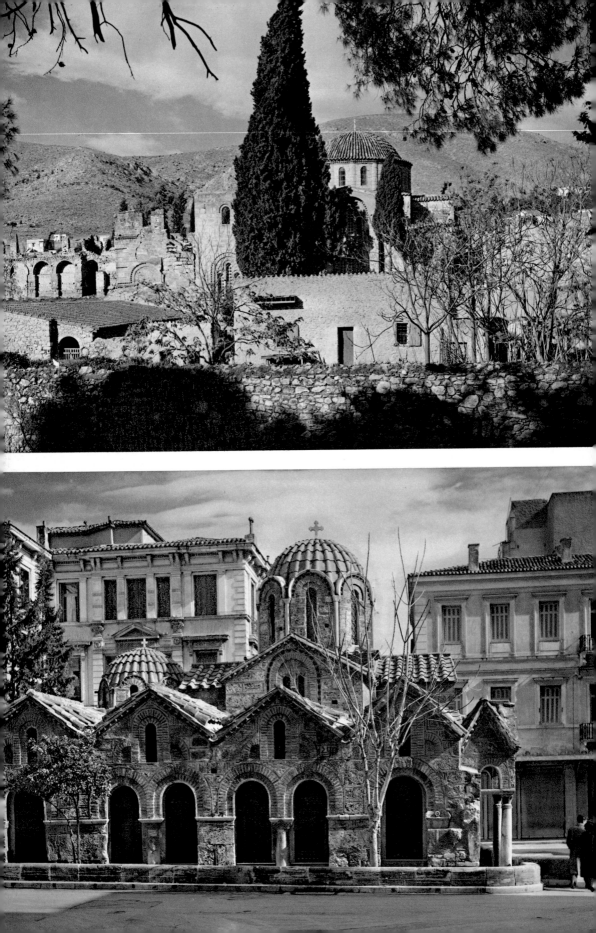

The large Temple of Demeter at Eleusis lies about $12\frac{1}{2}$ miles to the west of Athens, and here the ancient Athenians celebrated the Lesser Mysteries in February/March and the Greater in September/October. The Greater Mysteries lasted ten days. On the evening of the fifth day the torch-bearing procession moved from Athens to Eleusis, where the newly chosen were initiated into the rites of the Mysteries. The institution of the Eleusinian rites was said to be founded on a command given by Demeter to Eumolus to commemorate the blessings conferred by agriculture. The Roman Emperors expressed their veneration for the temple by adding new buildings, and even Pausanias guards the secret of the Mysteries, into which he was himself initiated, when giving his description.

The summit of the Acropolis, the ancient fortified hill at Eleusis, overlooks the sacred precinct. In the foreground, part of the hall of Philon, which stands in front of the sanctuary. To the south-east, the new town created by a number of industrial enterprises, and the bay of Eleusis.

Roman horse's head from the Eleusis Museum. It served as a support for a statue—probably of a Dioscurus—one of whose feet can still be seen on the pediment.

Eleusis.

66 The two crossed torches, the sign of Demeter, are depicted on many of the sanctuary's relief carvings. Here they ornament a base at the entrance gate, where the processional way led into the sacred precinct and the Romans built their great propylaea.

67 The detailed inscriptions on some of the pedestals outside the Temple of the Greater Mysteries tell of the dedicatory statues they once bore.

Already at the time of Homer, Cape Sunium (Cape Kolonnais), the extreme point of the chain of mountains bordering Attica on the south-east, was crowned by a temple visible from afar to seafarers who frequently encounter treacherous currents and winds off this promontory. The Temple of Poseidon of which twelve columns still stand today was built under Pericles somewhat later than the Parthenon to replace a sixth-century temple destroyed by the Persians. In contrast to the warm patina of the buildings built of Pentelic marble on the Athens Acropolis the columns at Sunium are of a gleaming whiteness; their marble may have come from the island of Naxos.

The little church of Ayia Triada stands at the foot of the Pentelicon, the mountain range rising to 3,604 feet north-east of Athens; the famous marble quarries that yielded the material for the most important buildings of Athens and for numerous Attic sculptures are situated within a short distance from it. In the small settlements in the pine forest the women weave in the open while the men work in the marble quarries.

The importance of Piraeus as port of Athens has increased with remarkable rapidity during the last decades. At a distance of just over six miles from the capital its 500,000 inhabitants make it the second largest town in Greece, with modern warehouses, factories, etc. When the liberation of Greece in the nineteenth century created the condition for this development only a few fishermen's huts stood in the place that first became important through Themistocles.

74

Marble relief in the form of a disk with the head of a goddess, dating from *c.* 460–455 B.C. and found at Melos. This important recent addition to the exhibits of the National Museum at Athens was presented by N. Kyritsis.